AF488879

Altruism

Reciprocity Not Needed

Michelle J. Jones

Copyright © Michelle J. Jones
All Rights Reserved.

This book has been self-published with all reasonable efforts taken to make the material error-free by the author. No part of this book shall be used, reproduced in any manner whatsoever without written permission from the author, except in the case of brief quotations embodied in critical articles and reviews.

The Author of this book is solely responsible and liable for its content including but not limited to the views, representations, descriptions, statements, information, opinions, and references ["Content"]. The Content of this book shall not constitute or be construed or deemed to reflect the opinion or expression of the Publisher or Editor. Neither the Publisher nor Editor endorse or approve the Content of this book or guarantee the reliability, accuracy, or completeness of the Content published herein and do not make any representations or warranties of any kind, express or implied, including but not limited to the implied warranties of merchantability, fitness for a particular purpose.

The Publisher and Editor shall not be liable whatsoever...

Made with ❤ on the BookLeaf Publishing Platform
www.bookleafpub.in
www.bookleafpub.com

Dedication

Status should never determine the level of love and respect that you show someone. Whether it be a CEO or a janitor, both deserve to have love and respect. My father Raymond G. Jones has demonstrated this to me throughout his entire life. He unselfishly has given love and respect to all those who has encountered and that birthed in me a belief in the power of altruism. The amount of love and respect that I have for my father can not be measured or contained. In appreciation to him, I dedicate this book to him. May God bless him on Earth and in his next life. May all the love he has poured into others, return to him.

Preface

Altruism is the act of showing others love. It does not seek to be self-motivated. It looks for nothing in return. It is performed because you are concerned with someone's well-being. It is shown through the love we give our family, friends, and humanity at large. Our ultimate model is the love God provides to us each and everyday. God shows us this type of love as he sent his only Son, to die on the cross to forgive us of our sins.

When Jesus was on Earth, He performed miracles, cared for the poor, lame, and misunderstood. His love for us was unselfish and never-ending. When He went to the cross, He gave us a gift. He did not go to the cross to gain anything for himself, but so that we may have everlasting life.

We live in a world, where many do not believe in Jesus as a Savior. However, He is acknowledged as a prophet and as an example of what love on Earth should look like. I think we all can agree that the message His expectation was that we love one another, care for one another, and provide provisions for those who are unable to. For the Christian believer, it is stated in 1 John 4:20-21 (NIV), " Whoever claims to love God yet hates a brother or sister is a liar. For whoever does not love their brother and sister, whom they have seen, cannot love God, whom they have not seen. And He has given us this command: Anyone who loves God must also love their brother and sister."

Christianity is not the only religion that has love as a core requirement. Love is the perquisite within many religions. Altruism can be cared out in many different ways into many different types of relationships. Love should never be conditional. Choosing to love someone does looses its power, when it is corroded by selfishness and malice. Can we truly say that we love someone, because they love us? What if the people we love, never show love for us, does that mean that we never show love to them?

Everyone is different, not everyone has lived a life similar as our own. Everyone has a different level of emotional intelligence. Some we considered enlightened, while others are to be considered sleeping. For those who are awake, it will be only natural to want others to experience love. Whether it be a religious mandate or something you decide to do out of your own experience or walk in spirituality, the spirit of altruism should arise.

The intent of this poetry book, is to celebrate, encourage,

and define altruism. Love is the greatest emotion we could every experience. Love heals and unites. It lifts up and sustains us through tribulations. I would never want to experience life not being loved or not being able to show love to others. I choose to love even when, I do not reciprocated. I choose to love because I love God. I choose to love, because I love myself. I choose to love, because humanities love bank is deficient.

Dear Reader, explore the reasons why you love and how you love. Love is a force that can wipe tears and change nations.

Acknowledgements

I would like to thank Beulah Heights University located in Atlanta, Georgia, for the education experience that I received from their great institution. Professor Betty Palmer, Professor John Nash, and Professor Carolyn Driver believed in me, when I did not believe in myself. They always provided me with encouragement and guidance. I wasn't the best student throughout my educational journey, but that did not deter them from showing me love. Beulah Heights University is a small private Christian University, with every course I took, I learned more about myself, more about God, and I will always accredit this University as the place where I learned to think. Memorizing and regurgitating facts does not always lead to cognitive development. The way my mind processes information, I need to be challenged and I needed to be shown how to wrestle with the text. Life application only comes when you can connect the fact with incorporating it into your life. My education at Beulah Heights University has immensely helped me to be a better person in and out of the marketplace.

I would also like to thank both of my parents. My mom has a zest for life that reminds me to work hard, but smell the roses along the way. My father's work ethic reminds me to work hard and always do my best. They scarified so much so that I could have a good life. They overcame their own hurdles, so I would be able to overcome my own. They didn't get a manual when I was born. I am sure they didn't know what to do all the time, but that never stopped them from being my parents. I was never abandoned or unloved. For that, I will always love and respect them both.

1. What Was the Cost?

God loving us, is always up for debate
Some only acknowledge Him, when we see destruction
and calamity
Others see a new sun rise, and the moon set and know
that God must exist
From the very moment of creation, He had us in mind
Do we consider what it must have cost

Whether we buy groceries
Care for our families
Give up our place in line
We can see the cost
Cost does not always derive from money
It can be paid from all sorts of resources
So what did it cost God to create us

God is God, He has all powerful
He chooses to love us, even when we don't love Him
At the moment he created man, He gave us free choice
He could have made it so we would always obey like
robots
It would have cost Him nothing

To give us free choice, I am sure it cost Him something

In the same sentence we say we love Him, he watches us
mistreat another
Does it hurt His feelings, when we discard and discredit
Him
He sits on His throne, and only interferes when He can
His word can not return to Him void,
He limits His own power, when His power is limitless
Could you imagine being an entity that restrains itself

His eye is in every place, He never sleeps, never
slumbers
What a thankless job, He only gets paid by our praise in
worship
He doesn't even demand a paycheck
He takes what He gets
I sure hope we are giving Him our best
He even released us from praise and worship
He made it so that the rocks will cry out in our absence

Any job we do, we expect payment
We expect something in return
Many don't get out of bed unless it beneficial
Everything demands a price be paid
Nothing is for free
What does it cost God to love us for free
There is no money exchanged and there is no fee

What can we do in return
How do we appreciate His sacrifice
We could choose to love others
Love them the way, He chooses to love us
Love is God's motivating force
Could it be ours
He already showed us, it cost nothing

2. Reciprocity Not Needed

You caring about me, I caring about you
Mutual Submission, Mutual Love is true
Reciprocity, gives to us both, but what if one can not give?
A helping hand, a warm meal
A place to sleep, clean clothes on ones back
In a vulnerable place, spirits swing low
Desperately crying out for help
Those that answer are willing
They look for nothing in return,
 this type of relationship is different
Nothing to be gained, nothing to be lost
Reciprocity Not Needed

3. I See You

I hope to see God's face one day
I hope to behold His beauty and splendor
Many years may pass until that day
Until then, I will look for Him in you
He created us in His very image

I will look upon your face
I will seek to see your heart
I will respond to your need
How can I love Him,
Without showing love to you

It's impossible to love Him
Without loving you
No one deserves agape love,
It is a gift that can only be freely given

4. The Plight of the Empath

Discovering you are an empath is a journey to responding to humanity.
Anyone can feel empathy, but not many respond to someone else's emotions.
At first you can't decipher between your emotions from another.
You are a listener by nature, but trying to fight against caring is like trying to take down a formidable city.

Emotions can run and high and they can be as low as a valley.
Feeling what someone else is feeling can bring you to your knees in prayer.
It is a plight, that many would rather ignore.
But your ability to feel deep things becomes your responsibility to respond with sympathy.

You will fight your own feelings of despair and naturally invite someone else's pain to rush through your senses.
Discernment kicks in and sometimes there isn't enough oxytocin available to keep both of you from crumbling.
But in time you will become steadfast, and you learn to help others see how to be self motivated to quieting their own storms.

The plight of the empath is not for the faint of heart.
You know you were created special to help others put a
label on their own chaos.
At times you feel like a social worker, always wanting to
help others to do better.
Other times you realize when to hold people accountable
to healing themselves.

A plight is a difficult situation but it gives us purpose.
Our periphal senses are far from being narrow, we
experience life being an intercessor.
We whole heartedly believe that oneness and wholeness
can be achieved.

We will hold the hand of people who hurt us, we hug
those who would never hug us in return.
It is a selfless experience, but one we still cherish.
The plight of an empath is more than a poem, it is a
signal to other empaths.

You are seen, when you feel invisible.
You are heard, when you think no one is listening.
And your appreciation to walk along side the hurt, will
come to you when you least expect it.
Don't stop, you are stronger than what you think.

5. The Invitation

As the sun sets and the sky becomes a blanket of stars
Your heart may wonder if hope and kindness exist
As a cool night's breeze glides across your skin,
you relish it as if you are being hugged.

You feel alone and isolated, singing songs of grief and
regret
Tears begin to run down your face
You feel unseen and unheard
But there is a place for you

Whether you know it or not,
 you are not a lone wolf searching for a pack
Don't give into despair,
each new day is an invitation

Although it is dark, you are a light and a beacon
The love you lack can be the same love you give
You know heartbreak and pain,
you can recognize it In the eyes of another
You have so much to give

Compassionate souls are needed
There is an open invitation, if you only accept it

Allow your pain to become your purpose
Helping wounded souls, will give you a reason
You have so much to give this world

6. They Were There Too

The streets cried out, injustice was all around
Hatred ran a muck and humanity was in crisis
Choosing what was right, was considered wrong
Crosses were being burned, nooses were hung
Segregated water fountains to segregates
Jim Crowe was barking as loud as dogs on the hunt
Black men, women, and children banded together
Marching up and down the streets
Sit ins and protest were the new normal

Like fireflies come out at night, new faces began to
emerge
First one, then two, then four, then some more
They were there too, they couldn't keep silent
The word injustice, unconstitutional, and integration
were no longer offensive to them.
The undertone of it, caused confusion
People whisper, chatter started, lines were drawn
They went from high society to only be asked, What do
you mean by those words?

While some white people turned up their noses
Others decided to turn down racist attacks
They held hands, with those who needed a hand

They were called names for standing up for the
oppressed
Their love for humanity was awakened to feel pass color
They didn't receive the same exact treatment,
 but they risked their privilege, and did all they could to
help the movement
They lost family and friends, some lost their lives
They were determined to stand up for what was right
No matter the cost, they chose to be of service
Their respect for equality knew no bounds
Determined to see change, they were there too

They were there to show compassion and empathy
Sung songs of freedom in unison
Tried to change the minds of their neighbors
In the fight to end Jim Crowe, we sometimes forget their
names
We forget the risk they took
God forbid we clump them in with those who did not
Because, they were there too

7. An Open Heart

There are broken hearts around the world
Hearts that don't care, caring hearts that do
Tenderness is taken for a weakness
Harden hearts mistaken for strength
So, where are the open hearts?
The hearts that are a bit torn, weathering away
Are the same hearts who decide everyday to care
Caring comes naturally, the pain inside doesn't
With a needle and thread,
Those same hearts mend the wounded
Band aids on top on band aids
Nothing diverts a open heart

8. Step Into the Water

Cool enchanted waters
Available to heal the body
Divine implicit memories
Never let go or doubt it
Ripples in water created by Angels
Scientists must agree and never refute
Submerge, allow the water to purify you
Step into the water
Healing is found in each ripple
Accommodating the masses.
Step into the water.

9. May We Recognize His Worship

He wakes up before the crack of dawn.
Hewalks over to the bathroom mirror.
He takes a deep breath and prepares to get ready for
work.
He is quiet much like the peace he feels in his heart
while making coffee.
Just by looking at this man, you would only think he was
going through his regular ritual,
but underneath his skin, through his muscles and veins,
he is mentally laying in a fetal position worshipping
God.

His worship may not look like anything we could ever
begin to understand but understanding that worship can
look like anything that is intended on connecting with
God in submission, is the kind of worship that God
wants.

The man then puts on his freshly ironed white button-
down work shirt, he takes another deep breath and, in
that moment, he is silently whispering to God, I love
you.
Worship doesn't need to be conventional, for it is the

ultimate medium to restoration and communion with the
Source of all your needs, wants, and desires.

At work, his boss treats him so bad, but the man
promised his son he would buy him a new computer. So,
instead of frowning, he shakes the other man's hand and
thanks him for employment.
In that sacrificial gesture, our main character
demonstrates self-control, patience, and appreciation:
character traits that are fruit of the Spirit.

If we as an audience could only hear his daily
conversation with God, we would know his worship is
more than just movements and gestures.
By 5 o'clock, it is time to clock out, the man walks by a
homeless family and gives them a few dollars. He looks
at the family and cannot ignore that, if he had not made
certain decisions that could have been his family lying
on the concrete and sleeping in cardboard boxes.

As the man walks away, he says a prayer for them and in
his own special way, He is not concerned with the fact
that those last few dollars were for tomorrow's lunch
money. His level of empathy was the product of him
making a promise to God, to always do His will which is
the ultimate key to demonstrating pure worship.

10. Hello Sister

Hello Sister, is it okay if I call you Sister?
We aren't bound by blood but we are bound by race.
Is it okay if I speak the truth in love and we talk about
the realities of the world?

No judgement, I believe we both have divine
assignments.
Can we speak on what hinders us from succeeding? Can
we speak on the moments that made us perserve and
cross the finish line?

Aren't we both on a journey to bring peace to the world?
Can we start with the peace that we both have within
and share how we can become peace makers between
others?
Can we collaborate and achieve more together than we
could on our own with no malice in hearts to sabatogue
progress?

Hello Sister, I just wanted to say, can we both shake the
world if we take turns jumping at different times?
I'm not here to harm you or to destroy your name.
When we all work together we can do some marvelous
things.

Walking together and working together will change our community.

Power alone is not enough when you need a network. Can I get a Hello…. to agreeing that relationships between women can be better than what's in the media? Let's stick together, work together, and improve the quality of life for every woman, man, little girl, and boy.

11. I, You, We

I, You, We
There is only so much I can do.
There is only so much that you can do.
But what we can obtain is immeasurable.
Engulfed in "I" statements, gives off narcissistic vibes, it hinders the movement of the spirit of collectivism like it's a yield sign.
Like a siren, an alarm should sound for those who are in need.

Its not about us individually, but it is what unites us that stops traffic.
Intertwining perspectives might cause quite the commotion, but together we form a ban of brothers who can contain it.
With the help of God, we can work together and create a bigger sense of community.
It's not about I.
It's not about you.
It's about what we can do together, it's about the synergy that can keep us in unison.
I, You, We

12. Deliverance

It would be so easy to cut you off.
All the pain that you have caused me or was it grief?
You made the wrong decision but we both received
punishment.
An ego that was swelled with false ambition, it gave you
a license to be foolish.

Escaping each moment that was meant to trap you, you
walked away free.
Warning was given, but you didn't listen.
Until the day that you heard the jail cell door close,
you had no real need for me.
You thought that you were invincible, but you weren't.

Watching you being sentenced, was one of the worst
days of my life.
As the judge spoke those words, I saw your soul
momentarily leave your body.
They then carried you away.
The only thing I could think of was that I wouldn't be
able to touch you for so many years.

I could either stand with you, or let you stand by
yourself.

Nothing could over turn your verdict.
Your plea deal was signed, sealed, and delivered.
Physically you would be imprisoned, but spiritually you
needed to experience an existential release.
Only God could help you, you needed to feel His
presence.

However, every time I spoke to you on the phone, you
weren't concerned with God.
You turned into the worst version of yourself.
Ungratefulness flooded your soul, you couldn't see any
reason to feel like you were blessed.
I didn't know what to do, but I prayed for
your deliverance.

When we were young children, we attended church and
heard how a condemned soul could be changed if they
were touched by the laying of hands, so I prayed my
hands could touch your temple.
I prayed that supernaturally my hands could be a vessel
extending God's power as a vehicle aiding in your
transformation.

I could have just stop talking to you, but how could i do
that?
I knew you wouldn't be able to be caged everyday for
years to come with you walking with Jesus.

You would have been consumed with negativity and
continue to turn into something I couldn't recognize.
My love for you would be required to longsuffer.

Each day i got on my knees and prayed for
your deliverance, even when you cursed at me.
I knew confusion was setting in.
I couldn't just stand by when I knew God could change
you.
I knew that God still had a plan for you.
I wasn't just going to let you waste away.
Although your words pierced my soul, I prayed that
God's love would pierce your hardened heart.

It would have been so easy to cancel you.
But, the right thing to do was to subscribe to the
opposite of division, eventhough it was hard.
I needed you to live, I needed you to feel loved. I needed
you to remember who you were before you chose to
make choices that landed you in this predicament.

I stayed dedicated to praying for your deliverance.
Eventually, you realized you needed God.
You accepted Jesus as your Lord and Savior.
Our phone calls became worship sessions, and I could
hear hope return to your voice.
God was with you as you served those fifteen years and

you gave Him glory as you walked out the gate.

Freedom was now your friend and you didn't turn back
to the life that brought you down.
You were a changed man, a true conversion that
committed their life to serving in God's kingdom.
Deliverance is soul work and when a person can't pray
for themselves, it is our responsibility to pray.
God always has a plan, cutting people off is not always
the best solution.

13. The Visitor

Days seem long when you are young
Running through the sprinklers
Dancing in the rain
Growing older feeling aches and pains
Watching family and friends transition
A full life will begin to feel so empty
Old age can be such a lonely experience
Waiting and wanting someone to talk to
Visits from those you know fades
You are left to sit alone until a visitor appears
Getting to know someone new
Staring at the opposite side
Looking into a new set of eyes
The visitor comes and reminds you that kindness still
exists
Someone to share coffee with
Someone to share a joke
Dying alone is no longer an option

14. A Stranger's Response

In this iridescent colored world,
We all must co-exist.
Although it may be unknown,
everyone is given a name.
Everyone has value,
we are all worthy.
I walk pass you each day,
We do not look the same.
We are but strangers,
who have crossed paths.
My cup is full of coffee,
yours is filled with change.
I decided not to judge you,
considering you have a story.
We both get on the train.
I'm not sure where you are headed,
but I chose to buy you a ticket.
You looked up at me and smiled,
I gave you a nod and smiled back.
We went into two different directions.
Looking out the window, as the scenery changed,
I hoped you made it to your destination.
I didn't need to know your name,
I didn't need anything from you.

I saw that you could use a helping hand,
I didn't ignore you, I responded.
If everyone did the same,
this world could truly be a better place.

15. The Heart of a Volunteer

Life without meaning doesn't mean much
It is such a thing to live a life of purpose
Storms may blow, the sun will shine
It will be up to you to account for your time
Without a grudge or a mumble
Without malice or contemptment
Morality should never be clouded by resentment

Dark clouds will fade, the fog will lift
A tough time is easier when you are near
You don't have to sacrifice much,
your time and labor of love can be given on purpose
Everyone needs a reason to keep going
Volunteering your time is precious
Selflessly opening your heart to another,
does make a difference

As the ocean crashed, and Jesus walked in the sand
He asked Peter three times if he loved Him
With each question, there was a command
Jesus wanted to make sure His sheep would be cared for
Yes, the poor will be with us always,
 but we must not become immune
We do it out of agape

A volunteer understands the ebb and flows of life
They give out of the love they have and
when they are out of love, they find a reserve tank
Clouds will glide across the sky, time will never seize
Neither will the love from the heart of a volunteer

16. Yesterday

Yesterday, I thought I wouldn't make it.
I thought life itself would end.
That morning, I sat at the edge of my bed,
it was like I couldn't even breath.
I sat at my desk, looking out the window
I felt like I was going to hyperventilate.
I decided to go for a walk through the park.
The wind blew across my face,
I could hear the birds chirping in the trees.
I wondered around the trails.
I sat down on a rock and the sun was bright.
It was like the sun rays gave me forehead kisses.
Mother nature was consoling me.
I continued my walk until I reached a stream.
I picked up a rock and held it in my hand
I found strength as I stuck my hand in the mud.
The dirt was wet and I starred to relax.
The elements showed me love,
asking for nothing in return.
I looked up to the sky and watched clouds passing by.
I started to use my imagination.
I allowed myself to cry, the trees were my only company.
I decided to trust the trees to keep my secrets.
I spoke to the leaves as if I was writing on paper.

I could feel love all around me.
No one in sight and I didn't feel lonely.
I felt at ease, I felt a true sense of belonging.
I was present and in the moment.
I closed my eyes, remembering only kind faces.
Nature provided me the elixir to ease my troubled heart.
If only connecting with humanity could be as simple.
A simple walk taught me so much.
When someone is in need, you only need to be available.
You don't have to give anything, listening doesn't require
a fee.
May I be like the rock I held in my hand,
Strong and sturdy, calming and nurturing towards
others.

17. A Kind Word

You saw me sitting
You saw my tears
You didn't ignore me
Thank you for your prayers
Kind words go a long way

18. A New Day

Each day is a day that we can not see again.
Once the day is over and the sun has set,
we wait for a new day to begin.
We start the day so hopeful, by the end,
we may not feel the same.
A new day brings new expectations,
everyone waits in anticipation for a new day.
Another day to show someone you care,
another day to demonstrate love and concern.
Let go of yesterday, and prepare for a new day.

19. Love in Different Shades

Love is more than a noun, it's a verb.
Love is more than a connection, to love is a choice.
Love is an action that can't always be defined.
Love is patient, love is kind, it's more than a theory, it's a
solution.

Sometimes we attract love that looks like our reflection.
Sometimes we attract love that is the opposite of what
we see in a mirror.
Sometimes we attract a love that can defy the odds.
Sometimes we attract love that is timeless.

No matter the shade or the hue of your partner, love is a
shared experience between two people.
No matter where or how the two of you met, both of you
deserve to experience love that is healthy and intense.
No matter if it matches our cultural background, it can
be ethnically different.
No matter if society approves, you can love whomever
you choose.

It is inevitable not to fall in love.
When someone chooses to capture your heart, whether
their eyes are blue or brown, you both deserve to be

happy.

If you prefer blonde, red, or black hair, it's your preference.

Love can come in different shades.

20. Thank You in Advance

Watching my father age is hard.
I remember him when he was a young man,
working so hard to provide for my brother and I.
He gave us so much love, I could never repay him.
Years have went by, I seen him loose his hair,
It even seems like he shunk a bit.
He is my hero, he sacrificed so much for me.
Now he needs someone to sacrifice for him.
His kidney has failed and he needs a new one.
Knowing he is tethered to a dialysis machine
3 times a week, is such a defeating feeling.
Wanting a donor to come forward,
would be a dream come true.
The reality is my dad will only receive one,
in the wake of someone's death.
Choosing to be an organ donor is a selfless act.
Choosing to give hope, even after hope is gone,
is a conscious decision of love, altruism at its very best.
Just imagine the day that a donor signs up,
they choose to give even when life is taken from them.
They choose to give away organs, to help others.
May one of these kind hearts, fulfill the need of a man,
who wants to live life, and complete goals that are on the
back burner.

Every person is a miracle, we are all surrounded around miracles.

My father is a miracle, who needs a miracle.

Thank you in advance for the miracle who decides to be a miracle, even when they are gone.

21. Defending Love

There are many different types of love.

Philos, Eros, Lupus, Pragma, Storage, and Altruism.

Each type has a different motivation, but each requires a choice.

Motivation can be reciprocal, and some motivation is not.

We each want to love and be loved.

Either it be romantic or brotherly.

Love is a most precious gift, it is delicate and intense.

Our first experience in love is from God, then family, friends,

humanity, and even seen at a nudge of a furry friend.

Love is a powerful force, we all are deserving of love.

Through romance, volunteering, or sharing a kind word, the act of love must be defended.

Hate can not swallow it up, prejudice must not burn it into flames.

The world requires love to freely move and we require it just like the air we breathe.

War will come and famine too, the poor will be with us always.

Family and friends all have love banks requiring deposits.

As a mother cradles their child, as a fallen solider is

honored,

as the environment changes, as an adult ages, as two
people share their first kiss.
Life would not be worth living, if there was no love.
It must be defended, we must choose to love.

www.ingramcontent.com/pod-product-compliance
Lightning Source LLC
Chambersburg PA
CBHW072050150726

47996CB00015B/2474